THE PANIC BIRD

Previous Poetry Publications

Fistful of Yellow Hope (Littlewood Press, 1984)
Cat Therapy (Littlewood Press, 1986; reprinted 1989)
Cathedral of Birds (Littlewood/Giant Steps, 1988)
Opening The Ice (with Ann Dancy) (Smith/Doorstop, 1990)
Crossing Point (Littlewood Arc, 1991)
Exits (Enitharmon, 1994)

MYRA SCHNEIDER

The Panic Bird

London
ENITHARMON PRESS
1998

First published in 1998
by the Enitharmon Press
36 St George's Avenue
London N7 0HD

Distributed in Europe
by Littlehampton Book Services
through Signature Book Representation
2 Little Peter Street
Manchester M15 4PS

Distributed in the USA and Canada
by Dufour Editions Inc.
PO Box 7, Chester Springs
PA 19425, USA

ISBN 1 900564 21 1

British Library Cataloguing-in-Publication Data.
A catalogue record for this book is available
from the British Library.

AUTHOR'S NOTE

It is coincidental that *The Panic Bird* is a term
Sylvia Plath uses in her diaries to refer to her anxiety.
The term is also referred to by Ted Hughes in
his *Birthday Letters*.

Set in 10.5pt Bembo by Bryan Williamson, Frome,
and printed in Great Britain by
The Cromwell Press, Wiltshire

Acknowledgements

Poems from this collection have appeared in:

Acumen, Agenda, Ambit, The Dybbuk of Delight: An Anthology of Jewish Women's Poetry (Five Leaves Publications 1995), *Frogmore Papers, The Inquirer, Lancaster Literature Festival Poems: 18, Navis, The New Statesman, The North, Other Poetry, Poetry London Newsletter, Poetry Wales, Principles of Art Therapies* by Daniel Brown (Thorsons 1997), *Quadrant* (Australia), *The Rider and the Rocking Horse: Harlow New Town 50th Anniversary Poetry Competition Anthology, Seam, The Swansea Review, Tandem, Writing for Self-Discovery* by Myra Schneider and John Killick (Element Books 1998), *Writing Women.*

'The Waving Woman' won 2nd Prize in The Sheffield Thursday Poetry Competition 1996; 'The Solitary Dog' was a prizewinner in the Lancaster Literature Festival Poetry Competition 1995.

'Need' was broadcast on *Woman's Hour* on BBC Radio 4.

Contents

Address / 9

Need / 10

Leavetaking / 12

Considering the Lilies

   The Lilies / 14

   The Waterfall / 17

   Recovery / 19

Taking Steps / 21

Waving a Wand / 22

Two Weeks in Trinidad / 23

Potatoes / 27

Stepping / 28

The Keynsham Church Poems

   Choir Practice / 30

   The Green Man / 32

   St Keyna / 34

   Material / 35

Generosity / 38

Elements / 39

Kingfisher / 41

The Convertible / 42

The Waving Woman / 44

The Solitary Dog / 74

Ablutions / 75

Woman in the Bath / 76

Freewheeling / 77

An Old Story / 79

Under / 81

The Red Cupboard / 82

The Panic Bird / 84

The Photograph / 86

Recuperation / 88

The Blue Balcony / 89

ADDRESS

Waking this morning, I fumbled
for the switch, that once-child
bright in my blurred head,
writing her name in joined letters
inside a bumper book
of the Grimm Brothers' fairy tales,

and under it two doorknocker fours
by Divert Road. Not interested
in going a long way round
she dived without pause to Gourock,
Scotland, then The World, THE UNIVERSE,
proud to fix her point in existence.

And possibility was a house of mirrors
where she shook patterns, unlatched
doors to islands, winged populations.
The need for success hadn't shut her in,
nor had she cried for love to stifle
loneliness, found it can hook, wound . . .

But when I got up this frostbound day
love was somehow my fleece lining.
And I saw the white midwinter moon
thin-skinned as the afternoon,
and myself a dot at the window
in a darkening room circling
a ball of fire in the universe.

NEED

(A postcard of Mother and Daughter *by Schiele)*

The mother is small-boned,
delicate as a folded bird.
Her long flamingo-red
off-the-shoulder gown
exposes the sad slant of her neck.

The daughter has not thought
to hide her nakedness: tight
twin buds of buttocks,
a narrow trunk. Impulsively
she hugs the quiet fire that wraps

her mother. Their heads touch,
mingle haystack-gold hair
threading from the same source.
Here is closeness beyond flesh –
each comforting, comforted.

The tenderness stops my breath
with a blade of pain that splits me
apart. In the gape is my mother's face
closed to mine, the silence
dividing us cold as glass.

And down a passage I make out
a dark-haired child – not me
but her. Blanks for eyes, she shrinks
from the woman whose pecking mouth
never sweetens with kisses.

In pale outline behind
the bitter woman is a girl
whose fingers flutter music. Duty
chains her to sickroom, kitchen,
rubs salt into her feelings . . .

So it goes back, must not go on.
I sift feathers of kindness, find
illuminating words, fill myself;
mark the place in my book
with the clasped mother and daughter.

LEAVETAKING

And when he was struck speechless
then I wanted him to speak again,
when he couldn't deliver the orders
I wanted to cram back into his mouth,
break the unbearable waters
of wrath over my head
then I wanted to hear his voice again,
would have held out cupped hands
for a command, a judgement, a complaint.

When he was sentenced
to a wordless struggle for breath
and could no longer devour us
with: 'I'm dying . . . I wish I was dead,'
I discovered what I'd guessed:
he'd cried wolf instead of pain,
stalked by implacable terrors
he dared not name. But he'd given
doctors instructions to haul him
back for the last mile, last inch

to keep tabs on the world,
its disgraceful conduct of itself,
his daughters' failings, successes
and the complex finances in his head.
Minutes before his lungs
finally rebelled
his fingers plotted in the air
the upward curve of a grandson's career.

And in those four days
when his eyes fixed
on the precise saline drip
drip through glass arteries,
when his hands washed themselves
of the universe or clutching at a pen
produced strange new writing,
did a kind of acceptance trickle through?

In those four speechless days
I began to strip him of shortcomings,
bury the terrible damages
and I hung onto his zest,
his generosities, his ever-
enquiring scientific mind,
his hunger for consciousness,
that miracle each person carries,
a delicate globe lit
by intricate, unseen filaments
which is so suddenly put out,
which is totally
irreplaceable.

CONSIDERING THE LILIES

The Lilies

1

April, and we're not in England
   with shut skies,
streaming roads, pavements squared off,
unimaginative, compassionless attitudes.
April, and I'm not crossing words out
or feeding them into mouthpieces of phones
or trying to funnel meanings
to someone whose speech was destroyed
   at a stroke
and most of her understanding,
who now keeps chalking the air
with wild messages I can't decode.

Footloose on the day's long track
   and high up,
the sun licking our sunhats, bare arms,
we sniff sweet peas and eucalyptus,
pick cow parsley twined with cactus,
pass through leafshadow beneath trees
tall as telegraph poles.

Suddenly we come upon the levada.
A limp old man, back umbered
by the weather, is dipping a bucket
in the shallow silver
   of its water.
His large Alsatian runs to and fro
   squandering energy.
I utter my single word of Portuguese.
His eyes flick over our absurd clothes
and wicker basket.
The earth flaked by heat, his arms

14

doggedly raising the small black bucket,
    persist.

2

We follow the levada
that threads this island with water.
It creeps across a hillside
where pink roofs flower among cramped trees,
vines border onion beds.
    Dark coops
in a yard, and someone with solid elbows
hanging a carpet over a white wall.
Bursts of geranium, cock crowing
unlatch childhood mornings
on rutted farm tracks.
And I pull such bunches of feelings
    from my heart
I can't hold them all.

Ahead, an immense valley created
by what boilings underground,
upheavals, gougings out?
Beyond it, mount fierce green terraces
and every plot is tilled,
    however small,
however sharply it's tilted to the sky.

3

A woman in a workaday brown skirt
to her ankles, hurries past
as we dabble in strips of sun and shade,
    gather pine cones.
A bundle of lilies wrapped in grained paper
is slung over her shoulder.

She has passed out of sight when we see
    the wild lilies
in their hundreds on the valley floor:
a fanfare of cool creamy bells,
their clappers, orange dots
that subdue long grasses and leafery.
Quiet unfolds its cloth.
These are the lilies of the field,
an array that surpasses Solomon's glory.
    In the brightness
I suddenly see Stanley Spencer's Christ,
a fat simple man, loose shirt billowing,
gentle face transfigured by wonder
    as on hands, knees
he contemplates small daisies.

And I know nothing matters
but this 'now' the unworldly Christ
rejoices in, this now
of the risen bucket, the ripened onion,
the carpet hung out to air,
the red crowing that unravels the past,
this now of the brain-damaged woman
putting her finger on my words
    and laughing;
this now of a dying playwright
as he looks out at pear blossom
    in April in England;
and the now of the figure with her goods,
a moving speck at the head of the valley.
I unfasten the wicker basket,
    fill it
with the silent clamour
from these open-mouthed lilies.

The Waterfall

Suddenly its icewhite head is butting
the blue midday heat that opens out
at the top of the horseshoe valley.
    Its bunched tails
      hang in tiers
which disappear inside the bowl
of the hill filled with dense green:
palms, pines, eucalyptus.

We've left behind plots with washing
blooming above paradise flowers,
dogs barking, cows hidden in huts.
    No roads for cars
      to nose out
this waterfall. We won't find postcards
curling in kiosks, beefburgers
stifling the scent of garlic, thyme.

The two of us will stand alone, voiceless,
as the quick liquid body gobbles,
chokes, clouds the air with its breath,
    slithers through
      rainbow jewellery,
hurls itself onto boulders. Mesmerized
by the roar we'll watch foam
blossom on bottomless cobalt pools.

Then I see the lily woman who passed us
not long ago, a pin-figure now
by a precipice, the cream flowers
    on her shoulders
      quite invisible.
When I pick out her fenceless path
and it dawns that we must follow it,
terror helter-skelters through me.

And I who always want to climb higher,
reach altitudes where gentians bloom
but can't look over bell tower parapets,
   forget dreams
   of silver falls,
examine a butterfly rimmed with orange
on the weed slime inside the levada,
the small water channel that dogs us . . .

A span of concrete steps. Far below,
a shrunken river struggling over stones.
I can no more cross this bridge
   than walk on air –
   but if I give up
I'd lose the glory of this adventure.
Sitting, I crab my way from slat to slat,
scrape wrists and knees, pause halfway.

I'm photographed with sunglasses
and smile covering my fear, at last reach
the other side, tumble into laughter.
   Ankles licked
   by cold water,
I paddle in the levada, pass the crest
of the fall, surefooted, without looking.
Swinging my plimsolls tied together,

I'm again the child who saw smoking stubble
as a forest fire and stamped it out,
set off on safaris through bog and bracken.
   I peer into
   rock recesses
at thin petals, at wrinkled cobwebs
shivering between giant fern fronds.
Waterspouts trill on my crown.

Recovery

Not here,
shrinking from a staring sheep
in a hoop of barbed wire
on the hill down to the village.
A priest's words intoned
to his Good Friday flock,
their rumbling responses, circle
overhead, magnified and cracked.

Not here,
thrust against a girl
with garnet nails who flicks
her charm bracelet. She jabbers
at a small man in a fawn coat
who smiles thinly. Train doors
slap and I struggle to inch
away from strange breath.

Not here,
sleepless in bed, eye
shielded by a cage. I try
to believe clarity will come –
am afraid my new lens
will never decipher bookprint,
read leafshapes in blurred trees,
eyes in fogged faces.

But if I concentrate
I can push myself back up
a steep island track, retrace
my path by the waterthread
of the levada, slither past
precipices, eyes averted, slip
under icy jets from springs,
and stiff with fear, feel
my way through three tunnels,
toes sliding on grit,

body pressed to cold
wet rocksides as I seek
day's reassuring eye.

Clear at last, feet
sandalled by heat, I'll come
upon green terraces rising
from a plunging valley.
And wild white lilies,
faces lifted to the sun,
will transfigure my world again —
here.

TAKING STEPS

Between whitewashed walls
smooth as seabird wings
your thick-stockinged legs
climb a fan of treads.
Not a crack for a flake of earth
to perch, for a seed to sprout.

The inevitable handscarf stifles
your hair. A funereal coat
silences your body. Below you
the fishing-mesh on the elbow
of road jutting over the sea,
is made of tesserae. At the top

in your salt-block house
where you clean, cook, clean
do you lean over beaten mats,
mutter at creeping vines?
Is prayer your balustrade
when blue morning bells?

What if you turn and buck
the work donkey, vault
the spotless walls? Would you
tear your legs on thistles,
run in crazy circles,
arms full of wilting plants?

Go down, risk the sea.
It's red as berry juice far out,
blood by the steep shore.
Don't shrink from the stony bed,
stinging cold, fast current.
Smell the sun.

WAVING A WAND

Instead of mangetout peas
they send a packet of pumpkin seeds.
You thumb one into a pot
and a seedling heaves itself up.
In June you discover a swelling
behind saffron petals.

Lifting the weighty globe,
you stagger up the garden steps,
enter it at the horticultural show,
win a ticket to the Grand Ball.
The charmed circle admits you
with wine, kisses. But the magic

that hummingbirds your heart
doesn't lie in diamond eyes,
feathered praise, glimmer in icefall
chandeliers, gilt-hooved settees,
in the papier mâché faces
of waiters ferrying vol-au-vents.

Magic shivers the straggly grass
in the quiet of the shrubbery
beyond open French windows
where you crouch with someone
too shy, too inexperienced
to offer trinkets of easy words

as you peer at a small reptilian head
caught in speckled light, remember
a toad shrivelled to leather
in a fruit net last summer, exclaim
at the single hop into night
and freedom, tremble when fingers
reach out to touch yours.

TWO WEEKS IN TRINIDAD

1

Not a dream – it doesn't wear off
after sleep though light eats
into everything hours before breakfast.
Nothing smells familiar.
Midday is clammy as stewed tea-leaves, evening
sweetened with jasmin and darker petals.
Nothing sounds usual.
Birds keep repeating their jokey calls
from the amazing heights of trees.
English is a foreign language with 'lahay',
'womb doctor', 'go'go', 'fire-one' –
and its rhythm makes fools of us.

Nothing we recognize in streets
of low clapboard buildings, verandas
edged with wooden lace. Our eyes feed
on unripe coconuts hugged together
high up trunks, palm spears ribbing sky,
heliconia with raised scarlet claws, orioles,
strawberry shirts worn with bodies
in every shade of black and brown.

We are pale – colourless as if necks,
fingers, ankles were kept behind shutters
and never touched, never blessed by sun.
The moment we stepped from Arrivals
into night's hustle, its syrup warmth,
stood among kisses, the moons of headlights,
babies, luggage spilling from trolleys,
I saw how strange we were in our whiteness.

But on the Savannah, in the fishmarket,
mall: smiles and 'Do you like our island?'
And on the afternoon we walk ourselves
to exhaustion the fat taxi driver we hail
is tickled pink by his joke: 'You come
from South Africa? I know you don't!'
Asks: 'Do they talk Cockney in Dover?'
Detours to discuss life with his wife,
tells us he has another in Guyana,
laughs a lot, charges us little.

Day by day we acclimatize. But as I stare
at the wind snaking through sugarcane fields,
at mangroves twisting into silty water,
as I tread endless sand by a restless ocean,
flee screaming from heavy black wings:
vultures or bloodsucking soucayants
circling, plunging to gobble skins;
as the sun's juice runs red across the sky
and we're warned: 'Don't go alone at night,'
a rolled-up tightness is always behind me,
excitement and fear lie inside me,
inseparable waters running deeper than dream.

2

Tonight our new friend, Rose Raschid,
is taking us to a party out of town
at the Senior Citizens' Birthday Club.
The limousine loops past foliage
smothering roofs, and through my head
slide metal teapots in village halls,
shapeless dresses, dancing. We stop
by a bungalow with no outer walls.
Rupert Granger, retired police superintendent,
straight as a post, wearing the uniform
he's preserved for years, welcomes us gravely.

Indoors, light silvers his black skin.
'The fairy godmother has come with guests',
he informs the rows of quiet clothes,
lined faces. I cringe at the clapping.
Party? This is speech day – my husband and I,
V.I.P.s, are led to the long table in front.
I want to protest but in this nightmare
we've turned into British Imperialists,
our Jewish ancestry no excuse.
And I can't wipe out the six iron links
that once shackled ankles, now hung
like a loop of jewels behind museum glass.

A prayer. Then Rupert Granger who rules
his flock with a voice of steel, offers a vote of thanks
to Rose who introduces my friend from college
in a different life decades ago.
Diplomat now, she eulogizes birthdays,
asks to spend hers here, is cheered.
Without warning Rose invites me to recite
my poems but all the lines crumble.
I snatch at words and my head fills
with tulip trees, humming birds, orchids
nested on rainforest trunks. Sentences
float from my mouth to a carnival of smiles.
The table begins to dissolve.

The gift-wrapped prizes are readied
and a man in the back row stands:
'I'm proud to be here. My grandfather
was little more than a slave.' I'm close
to tears but the senior citizens sit unmoved.
They've worn stories like this next to the skin
all the days of their lives. Each birthday winner
is called up to shake hands with a guest;
one half-curtsies but Rupert, last
on the list, gives me a robust kiss.
The Ritz with all its grandeur and glitz
couldn't create such a sense of occasion.

The ceremony ends and all division
from the audience. I talk to Anita
who often flies to London, loves crossing it
on buses to visit her different nieces;
to three ex-teachers who ward off loneliness,
its wolf eyes, by phoning one another. No need
to say life is made up of these small links . . .
'You've never stewed bananas?' Half-way
through the recipe it's good-bye time.
'Come back,' they press with voices, hands.
We promise. Outside flower scent is feral
and Rupert is aiming his camera.
From behind glass we wave at faces.
Night springs at the car as it moves off,
doesn't disturb the island curled inside me.

POTATOES

Not exhibitionists like brash peppers
cockadoodling red, no dark frills whispering
into pale caps, not the tapered glow of carrots;
waistless, without a soupçon of style,

not even the surprise of an enormous arm:
green stripes plumped on friable earth
under leaves so coarse they draw your blood –
these thicken on stems which worm whitely

through a stony dark among the rods
and hairs of root systems, ant colonies.
Sub-cinderellas with scabby cheeks,
they are never given a chance to sparkle.

But after the prizewinning, the partywhirl
all night when scarlet fizzles from binned petals
and yesterday's sound bites bite the dust,
take this plainspeaking apple of the ground,

put it in the oven. Wait while it sucks in heat,
swallows the cold at the foot of the stairs,
crown the softness in its jacket with needles
of cheese, plant its solidity in yourself.

STEPPING

from the hassle of Piccadilly
into St James's churchyard,
midsummer netting my hair,
head thick with sleeplessness,
I'm caught up in a snare
of brightness, sit on a bench.

Out of sight voices argue
but I'm entranced by water arcing
from the mouths of stone fish
held by cherubic boys.
It plitters into a stone dish –
and suddenly the two are there,

bodies earthy but faces
so utterly white with age
on a day plaited with gold
I shiver, remember the silk
of a purse in a tissue fold,
how time has discoloured it.

Backs stately, the pair rest
on my bench. 'Shocking!' they agree
when a figure, long hair
feathered with scraps of material,
appears and a policeman bare
from manly elbows to fingertips.

'I love you,' sings the creature –
actor in a comic dream? On cue
the constable's: 'I love you,'
and the taller's: 'Help me, dear,
I'm nearly ninety-two!'
The officer gently raises her.

'I hope I'll walk London
at such an age.' Dazed, I stand.
'You will, dear,' they assure.
I follow the frail dauntless steps.
And their white heads endure
down months of Piccadilly.

KEYNSHAM CHURCH

Choir Practice

   for Elizabeth

Dusks and darknesses come together
with light to make music:
strike triangles on panes,
draw harp strings across floors,
pour brightness in high arias
from the choirstalls into the nave.

Silent in a pew, I wait
for the choir to begin, uncertain
where the voices will lead me.
Above, pink–gold branches
twist, gleam, echo. Once
they bore buds of fragile fire. Now

each flame, unwinking behind glass,
could stare me out. I try on
the confidence of Mrs Ann Tillie
who gave the chandelier and believed
the wealth she bequeathed would pay
for candles, for yearly cleaning forever.

The choirmistress, notes pitched
in her head, gathers faces
at her finger ends. Among the choristers
I see a woman shrunk with age,
a boy of eight shiny as the ball
he's just bounced down the aisle.

Singing layers the air:
silks of sopranos fluttering
over furs and weighty brocades.
And I'm back in the school choir,
wearing my serge skirt from years ago,
voice surging from its box

to join the single body moving
through space with the ease
and purpose of a bird in flight.
The choir gives me definition
when I have little, a place
to fit when I've nowhere to belong . . .

'Were you there when they nailed him
to the tree?' The anthem soars
above the chancel arch. Not a Christian,
not a follower of any religion,
yet I share bewilderment, guilt,
think of self snuffed, sacrificed,

hooded ash-points on branches
death has stripped. A man in glasses
and a dark jacket sings alone,
his notes dramatic with agitation.
At the church door which is open:
banging and tattered jeering.

Who comes to rip the raiment of music,
to thieve us from ourselves?
Unwavering, the soloist heralds
a turning point. As the shouting fades
the organ begins. Its huge waves roll
through the nave, through stone walls.

From the choir rows singing rises again,
grows immense. The small self
sheds its boundaries, widens, deepens
like a muddied puddle that suddenly holds
blue sky, mountain ranges of cloud,
the white circle no eye can rest on.

The Green Man

At first I can't make out heads
in the snake-weave of stems
and fluent tongues that curl upwards.
But in the screen's corners
they emerge suddenly from the dark
of oak: two human faces,
carved mouths speaking leaves.

A hare-leap of recognition –
yet I can't decipher these words,
find myself (minutes later,
or is it months?) in a wood, its quiet
thick as green needles overhead,
papery ghosts underfoot,
insistent as the damp that spawns

panther cups. And I'm on the track
of a past antlered with branches,
follow it through creeper darkness
to a stream trickling between banks
where a bush holds out scarlet hips.
Tyres swish as I cross and the trail
thins to a thread, is snapped

by a motorway. Puffing poison
it rushes me to an immense city
of glass storeys, concrete struts.
Bereft, I enter a store, stare
at slim refrigerators, satin blouses.
Voices offer me the world: its wildlife
on video, its wisdom on disk.

I cannot live on these things,
must breathe the cool of leaf,
feel its skin between my fingers.
In here the air is sickly
with perfume, the light strident
from a thousand bulbs. How far
to green layers that filter sun?

Shouldering doors, I push my way out.
And now the heads crowd round me:
a maple-lobed countenance;
eyes and nose daunting behind
an acanthus mask; a face
that's fruited in a plant's hub; a smile
curling from a leafery of beard.

How the differences between
bone and wood, leaves and flesh
are rubbed away. Sap mingles
with blood, fills capillaries.
In my street, at my desk, in dreams
I uncover faces on wooden screens,
touch on the truth their mouths speak.

St Keyna

A princess but she refused
to marry. Eighteen and intense,
did she see a vision in beds
of watermint, hear a silence
beyond bees humming in foxgloves,

or was the sacred state a way
to escape frequent births
with death mouthing at her side,
to gain space to follow
unending serpentines of thoughts,

time to feel the leap
of cool green leaves,
the heart haring wildly,
to reject a world where cruelty,
clothed in purple, crushes?

Fed up with her suitors,
the fine nothings of their words,
an inner voice spurred her to face
the night, its huge darkness,
sudden whirrs, frantic cries.

In small boats she crossed
the hissing Severn and Avon,
found 'a certaine woody place',
was undeterred by devil's fingers
growing on stumps, slitherings.

When she asked the local chief
to let her dwell in its solitude
he warned the place so swarmed
with serpents neither man
nor beast could live in it.

Keyna spoke, and her tongue
filled the dumb air,
quietened fears, stilled
the snakes squirming in mud.
Their coils can still be seen

stamped on Keynsham's walls:
complete ammonites, capacious
as dinner plates, dustbin lids,
one traced among vein blues,
dove pinks on the church.

Fact or fiction, Keyna knew
words can sound loud
as bells, go deep as wells,
weigh more than gold, discover
wings emerging from a cocoon,

shore legs from flippers,
the moon's monthly seepings;
that when life shrivels
and only its shell remains,
words continue to speak.

Material

'Miss . . . miss?' A flock of small
unsettled birds, their questions
circle, excite the air.
For many this is a venture

into an unknown where arches
swerve far above their heads,
stern walls are laden with notices
and the furniture makes no sense.

But this is not a dip
into religion. Their teacher
has asked for a guided tour
of the materials in the church.

Not chivvied to be quiet, warned
to keep their everywhere hands
to themselves, they touch shinings
from suns, knobbles in leaves,

palm the cold stone of pillars
giant arms could reach round,
open wooden doors to seats
Miss calls pews.

She reveals gold threads
in a silken cloth, traces
a glass man dressed in a glory
of red, feet on a glass carpet,

points to branches overhead
that turn into molten stems
with flowerets bright as stars.
And wonder holds them until

shocked by the news of bones
buried beneath their feet,
they gasp, picturing white skulls
with grins, fishbone spines,

and rush past alabaster stares
to look at metal pipes
stiff as a row of soldiers
behind keyboards and stops.

Children, from the organ
such fabrics of sound unroll:
rich rug textures,
layers soft as lawn

which join edgelessly with the rise
and fall of singing voices,
the light lying in swathes
on these much-trodden floors.

In this place too, finer
than filigreed silver, finer
than spiderthreads: the silence
which illuminates feelings, thoughts.

GENEROSITY

At first you rejoice in the amplitude:
room opening into high-ceilinged room, the gravity
of leather in the library, the shine on newel posts,
views from your turret. Wandering into the garden
you marvel at artichoke heads sprouting
thistles, onions bulging beside marrow trumpets.
In the greenhouse a transistor playing Vivaldi
to heavy tomato clusters enchants you.

Re-entering, you notice gilt crucifixes
long as daggers at every turn and red slashes
across cigarettes which shout: 'Thou shalt not!'
An elderly woman barks you into the herd
she's driving into the Victorian dining-room.
In the grey hush she intones grace gracelessly.
At a refectory table you suffer two fishcakes
in lurid jackets, peas from the freezer,
the director's welcoming speech: a timetable
of his holy life rolled up with intricate instructions
for locking doors and slapped in your face.
You reject the smell of righteousness
but it sours thoughts, seeps into notebooks . . .

At home in your cluttered suburban kitchen
you sit eating doorsteps trickling honey, finger
the jar that collects up light, returns without stint
a series of glinting ellipses, pinhead suns. Licking
sweetness you recognize what you believe in
is laughter, arms held wide, the kiss
of kindness that succours the first feelers,
supports stems, nudges open petals.
Yours is a creed of auburn shall, crimson will.

ELEMENTS

I thought you swooped on fly-
clogged, midsummer pools
where water irises crowd
and weeds with wild green arms.

But long past the year's apex
I'm surprised by your helicopter veer
and buzz as you patrol this docile space
hugged by posts, rooves, traffic-clatter.

You whose life begins in water,
ends in air, I envy your ease
in both elements. Nymph
in the cool and fecund ooze

at the foot of the pond, maturing
for a year or more until the moment
you climb a reed or lily pad,
unrobe from childhood, lift

into light and lightness beyond
imagination for a flawless month,
then cessation, a leaf flake
falling into night.

No lost vision, pester of feelings,
decline into age, its grey malaise.
No urge to plough the earth,
bore into it, rob it of goodness.

I want to be a blur of wings and blue,
see in all directions, a creature
who'd found an equilibrium long
before humans footed the planet,

until I realize I'd lose
the power to marvel at insects,
wouldn't even know your names:
darter, hawker, emperor – dragonfly.

KINGFISHER

You led me past a white
untidy flock of honesty across
your lawn to a stream, said:
'The kingfisher comes in May.'

Ceaseless tongues of water,
a frothing over stones – I thought:
if I part iris stalks for a month,
I'll never see the sudden wings

bluer than midnights in June.
The bird will always fly through
the darks between leaves, perch
on a cool twig outside my sleep.

Why not settle for other blues:
bright-eyed speedwell, scabious –
its buttonheads dotting chalky grass,
the turquoise sea, speckless skies?

Why the shiver of excitement
as if the fisher epitomized revelation,
the height of love, as if sighting it
was a key to living more fully?

Besides, the bird is no paragon.
The plumage warns of a taste
that is foul; the fish it bangs to death
on a branch it swallows in a silver slither.

So why do I comb your stream,
my reasonable clothing discarded,
why do I write at your table dreaming
of that burning blue moment?

THE CONVERTIBLE

Backs turned on the snow skins
lying thinly over the park grass,
two Parcel Force vans are stealing
a few quiet minutes together
as they always do at one o'clock.
Posed on the frozen sludge
at the end of the parking space:
a new crimson convertible,
hood folded – a hibiscus bloom.
Its pistil is a yellow-headed girl
in a summer jacket. Beyond her:
the sun caught in a net of twigs,
the viaduct's cathedral complex
where promise sifts endlessly
through a violet tunnel of arches.

Patients stranded in waiting rooms,
guests half asleep in hotel lounges,
will kill time by glancing at the model
perched on top of the driver's seat
in a car spread over a double page.
None of them will see the breath
steaming from the mouths of men who joke
as they set up cameras, or note
how they focus lenses to suggest
July warmth rising from the grass.

None will see the parcel carriers,
red lovers who keep silence
under the third viaduct arch,
or the two magpies now alighting
on the path by a cracked-ice puddle,
or me wondering at the instructions
invisible to naked eyes,
which reproduce and reproduce
those arrogant tail feathers,
that jewel-blue glitter on the wings.

But eyes looking through a lens
that magnifies a thousand times
a speck of paint from a car
or van, a flake of human skin,
would enter a land scaped by huge
honeycomb formations, bristles standing
stiff in sculpted forests, lines
ending suddenly at ravine lips,
come face to face
with the particles of matter
that make up our world.

THE WAVING WOMAN

One

Not a twitch of light on the line
but far along it in the darkness
train rhythm is petering out. Jumpy
as a cat, Rebecca turns. Not a cough,
a lit clockface, a destination.

The cold could be a hand
sneaking up her skirt. And already
she can see Thomas looking up
from a wad of papers stamped 'Order
and Safety',

               hear his irritated
'Why didn't you call a cab?'
and herself apologising, not able
to say taxi drivers unnerve her.

By the exit she listens – silence
in the booking-hall's plastic bubble.
Street noise, the Spice Palace
where she and Jade feasted on hot
coriander chicken – moments out of reach.

A distant sound-dot grows
and the rails become manic icicles.
Doors open. Warmth seals her in.

Who is this poised woman smiling
in the window-blur? The velour hat
framing an almost prettiness
startles Rebecca

who sees herself
as nothing special, her only gift
the words she feeds to those
who grew up wordless, those
who were suddenly shut out of language
and left babbling syllables of nothing.

'Something about you makes me think
of still waters,' Jade had said once
when they were snatching minutes
at the Unit to pool ideas
about the problems they tried
to ease – Jade with paints, crayons,
she with deaf signs, words on cards.

Tonight Jade was so unlike the woman
who'd encouraged patients all day.
She'd talked volumes about her life,
its downs and ups,

                    and half envious,
Rebecca was shaken by a vision
of herself as a buttoned parasol
that hadn't opened out . . .

                    Now, the face
in the window is echoing her dullness.
She waits tensely for her station,
bounds up steps that clatter the cold,
leaves her ticket at the empty booth.
Hurrying home,

she imagines Thomas
in a worn jumper, eating the casserole
she'd made, oblivious of its taste
as he reads a parliamentary report
in the paper, then surprised to find
the lounge chill because he forgot
the radiators, warming himself with a gin.
She prickles at the predictability.

By the park's broken railings
she's half afraid arms will pull her
into the bushes so she hugs the kerb.
Frost crystals cover the pates of cars

but one has the huge black gleam
of a dolphin she once watched
in a pool from a subterranean window –
its easy grace as it dove, swam,
rose. Propelled by excitement
she'd entered its fluid world.
Is it the memory

        of vaulting into
another medium that makes fences
walls, pavements, edges melt? –

As if she's a fish unrestricted
by cold scales she swims
through streetlight, moonlight,
as if a bird not confined by feathers
she flits below, beyond air.
Exultant, she flows past gates,
past flickerings from screens
planted in solid sitting-rooms.

When she opens the front door
the darkness makes no sense
and at first she can't take in
the casserole still in the oven,
the absence of his briefcase, voice.

Two

Throwing off her anorak,
Jade swears at the bookmuddle,
the rucked African throw
on the sofa, some rotting apples.

When Rebecca had praised this mess,
asked to see her paintings
it was as if she'd switched on a heater.
Up in the makeshift attic studio
she'd gasped at the unfinished portrait
of Surinder from the Unit:

                  'It's brilliant –
a flowerhead of fawns, cinnamons
and umbers and yet so exactly her –
I love those bright-seed eyes.'

'I drew her while she was pointing
at a page of scarlet and canary circles
and letting out those waterfalls of sound.'

Still in a glow at the Spice House
Jade had ordered lavishly, then pouring
wine, asked: 'Did you know
my rotten husband skedaddled
when the twins were eight? He belonged
to my naive period.' She can still hear
her over-dramatic:

                  'Some days
that winter every minute hung
like a stuck pendulum, and for a week
it was cold as a bloody morgue
when the electricity was cut off.
To me candles still stink of poverty.'

Rebecca had drawn her out
and she'd talked too much
about her first exhibition
and her gentle lamb of a lover,
but hadn't mentioned he was married –
only seeing him in dribs and drabs.

Snatching her sketchbook, she pictures
Rebecca's quiet brown hair, face,
speculates: is that innerness simply
a melded-to-husband look?

                      'Belt up!'
She begins to draw her friend,
forgets everything but the pencil
shaping, shading kind eyes, the give
in her shoulders, the waver in her mouth.

Three

It's two hours since the committee
on crowd control limped to its end.
His secretary's taken her cough home.

He enjoys the solitude, preparing
for the committee tomorrow, knows
his choice examples will make an impact:
a knife attack on a cripple, an arsonist
aged eight.

           As he locks his papers up
he glances at the family photograph:
Sue at twelve, face shining,
fair hair not yet chopped, purpled,
no saxophone, drum-mad boyfriend.

And Rebecca girlish but so much
less vague then than she is now –
always losing one of his socks
in the wash, bleating stupid sorries.

He notes the subdued cardigan
over a chair in the outer office,
nods at George downstairs, on guard
in his glass box.

                    As the streetdoor
slides he steels himself against
the smack of cold, takes a short cut
down an alley where a lamp sheds
light on the gummy eyes of a girl
wearing the label: 'HUNGRY'.

Badgered by figures of the homeless,
he directs the beggar to a charity shelter
but, stoned or deaf, she ignores him.

At a loss – she'd waste money
on drink or drugs – he moves on,
tutting to himself: seventeen, less,
sees Sue, her blare swallowing up
his words. Pauses . . .

At home a casserole is simmering.
He'll tackle *The Times* crossword
in the comfort of his dressing gown.
In two minutes an electronic mouth
will suck in his ticket.

He turns.
The girl could be a package
cluttering the doorway. Her blanket
stinks. Don't stay here . . .
what's your name? Words insist
in his head but instead of speaking
he searches blindly in his pocket,
presses a few pound coins into her hand.
Slowly she opens out her palm.
Scratchy sounds emerge from her throat.

Running. His arms are pinned, his wallet
prised. He kicks, hears her scream
beyond brimming faces.
He's struck. Black circles
flower in his head, drown him.

Four

A teddybear is jammed head first
into a box and plastic boats
are strewn on the cord carpet.
Jade stares through the glass panes,
can't shrink the relentless corridor,
quieten the throb of the heating's breath.
How can patients be healed here?

Time was confiscated at the door.
It could be ten minutes – hours
since a summoning nurse appeared,
chest flat as an ironing board.

Eager to caricature the awkwardness,
she hunts through her floppy bag
for her sketchbook, then remembers
she'd tucked it under a cushion
when Steve tapped at the door.

After parking his dog in the kitchen
with a large plate of 'crunchbites',
he'd held out a pot from the hothouse
where he kept spring and summer alive
all winter.

As she fingered the dark
green petals taut as bird beaks
he'd cupped her head in his hands,
muttered: 'Minus five tonight,'
worried about his cyclamen, cinnerarias.

And she had pictured frost singeing
the magnolia skin of the invalid wife
who'd punished him all evening.
If questioned he always quoted the hours
of pain she'd suffered, then clammed up,
so Jade had put her lips to his neck.

How easily they'd peeled off
the day's stains, its ragged edges,
lain naked and new in a warmth
brighter than any colour
she could mix on the palette.

He had held her buttocks, called them
firm apples, kissed the small
of her stomach until it melted
and she'd known again touch was more
than sight, smell, sound.

Yet (not for the first time)
she had torn their closeness,
its delicate tissue, insisted
they fitted so exactly it was wrong
to live apart,

then thrown out:
'I'm not a plant in the park you tend,
to be patted daily and fed twice weekly.'

Final as secateurs, he'd clipped:
'You know I can't leave June –
she's sick,' and within minutes,
face padlocked, he had gone.
She had smashed a mug against
the back of the futon, promised herself
to unroot him from her life
when the phone cut through the emptiness.

Not him – Rebecca incoherent
about burnt food and missing husband.
She had almost hooted: 'Men –
past masters of the vanishing act!'

Didn't. Black coffee. By the time
she'd de-iced the car, driven round,
the police had located Thomas Coombs.

Five

Temples bandaged in white,
face so stiff, so bled of colour
it could be a plaster cast,
he twists the sheet and shifts.
Rebecca fishes 'hurts', 'papers',
from the stream of slurred complaints.

At last Thomas registers her presence.
'Sue?' he shakes his head.
With forced calm she takes his hand,
strokes it. 'No, dear, it's me –'

'Fly it!' He flicks her off,
hasn't any idea who she is.
To keep a grip on herself she tries
to fill in the skeleton of facts
the police gave her,

                    guesses he stayed
at work extra late as she was out,
and compiling policies in his head,
stopped, started, muttered on his way
to the station – easy to rob.
So why fell him with a stone?

The bed tilts, the bald walls
swing with faces that feed on violence.
She tries to summon up the brace
of constables alerted by a girl
who screamed

               but only sees herself,
a hen panicking home, certain
he was a secure fortress. Guilt
rushes through her, bangs doors.

His eyes are closed now and she prays
that sleep will end his confusion
but as she replays the doctor's guarded:
'Too early to assess the damage,'
the fear she's nursing, swells.

'Pain in my belongings!' yells Thomas
bringing Sister Carey with a red
carnation smile and a syringe.

'Just a pinprick, Mr Coombs',
she urges in a squeaky-doll voice,
then to Rebecca: 'He'll rest now –
you go home, tuck yourself up.'

Six

Silvery rivers of roads unravel
from darkness, hiss as other passers
in the night loom. At a roundabout
Rebecca gives directions.

'Shit!' says Jade as they swerve,
'no gritting,' but each is thinking
of brain-damaged clients at the Unit,
and Rebecca sobs: 'I'm so afraid!'

'Don't cross bridges,' Jade urges,
'keep your strength for making cocoa,'
stems apologies and gratitude.

Home at last, Jade hugs her,
bucks up the drinking chocolate
with brandy, makes her giggle,
shares the king-sized double bed
and within moments vanishes in sleep.

But Rebecca, tensely awake,
is invaded by a monster Thomas,
garrulous, irritable, struggling
to retain fragments of information,
pensioned off, unoccupied . . .

For an hour a week it's easy
to soothe a person whose thoughts
are tangled, extract a few meanings
but how do you bear it

                          if the man
you've lived with for twenty years,
who manages the money, the decisions,
turns into a confused and angry child
you can't control? Suddenly
she's furious she's been so dependent.

The half hours lumber by
and sleep is a woolly place
out of reach.

Morning begins:
traffic tearing across the darkness;
scenes she can't prevent unfold
inside her head: Thomas referred
to the Unit,

Surinder, hands shaking
with excitement, showing her pictures;
he condemning the gaps in faces
and incomplete tubes of bodies.

'You mumblebrain!' the voice has turned
into her father's and when his fist hits
the green baize of the card table
she's appalled to see the inky mess
of her maths homework among bills,
forms, sheets of instructions.

Powder colours are pouring into
her nostrils. If she could flounder
to the sea

she'd dive to clarity,
rise again, float freely.
She tries to scream. Jade's voice
hushes in her ears, unsmothers her.

Seven

The sun alighting on panes
strikes rods, rhombuses, stars
with a thousand spokes in matter
that quivers, has no substance
yet is more intense than glass.
The radiance overhead lessens

the deadweight Steve is lugging:
the supervisor's malicious glint
as rolling a mean pinch of tobacco
he'd eyed the purple cinnerarias,
thrown out: 'The hothouse is a luxury
the council may have to give up.'

And in the moist heat where winter
is defeated Steve leans over
the sweet-scented jonquils,
recuperates from June's razor words,
from hours of fetching and pacifying.

He touches dark succulents,
the softness of dotted tongues
no human being could invent.
Here with the plants

                    he is himself,
knows the way they breathe, move,
revel in space, create silence.
Can only recapture this sense
on nights he needn't cut short walks
with the dog, nights June's pills
draw her quickly into sleep

and he's free to watch Torch leap
into drifts of wasteland grass.
These were the times he went on
to Jade whom he's loved

                    from the day
he came upon her by the park lawn
wheeling an Indian woman headscarfed
in mauve, heaving her to her feet
to let her clap at parrot tulips
and wave at herself in the boating pond.

Ten minutes from his house
to Jade's flat, its easy clutter,
her paintings that amazed him: a city
spanning the interior of a head, trees
like arms raised in supplication.
And she fed him with talk, kisses,
listened, released him
from the narrow plot of his life

but smashed his happiness to bits
whenever she said June's illness
was her own fault or worse, shouted:
'Your wife would survive without you!'

It's five days since she's barred him
from her flat and her anger's so hard
he's afraid it won't melt.

                    Helpless,
he peers at the fish, flicks of gold
in the miniature pool, goes out
through two doors, is blinded
by light exploding on pond ice.

Eight

'Stop flapping – go back
to work tomorrow. He won't die
of loneliness if no one visits.'
Sue's voice, hair, bangles,
perfume, overwhelm the kitchen.

Turning the cold tap full on,
Rebecca washes cherries for Thomas.
Her daughter's grand gesture –
coming home to help –

                                  is forgotten
for a gig rehearsal. She seems
untouched by the danger he's been in,
unaware he may not recover fully.

Sue takes a handful of cherries,
puts two in her mouth, spits
the stones: 'This is your chance
to stop pussyfooting round Dad,
pandering to all his whims,
get liberated . . . '

'Shut up!' escapes from Rebecca.
Something hot and unstoppable
passes through her throat

and as if unconnected with her
screaming bursts into the kitchen,
pierces the cold garden.
She makes no attempt to staunch
the sound and when it dies
she doesn't apologize to Sue
who's stonestruck by the table,
instead croaks:

'Go – leave me alone!'
'Fuck you!' The girl rushes out.

It's then as she tries to grasp
the stillness that Rebecca notices
she snapped a tumbler in two
banging it down on the draining board.
She cuts her finger putting the pieces
in the swing bin and, legs weak,
sinks onto a chair.

                    The trickles
on her hand could be cherry juice,
remind her of walking over grass
towards the sun's crimson ball.

For a moment she sees the Unit
hemmed in by towerblocks, bridges
and old terraces shaken by traffic,
the nearby park an oasis of quiet
with flowers always in bloom.
But her mother

                    intrudes with a trug
of plants, face rigid as a trowel
while Rebecca trails behind with years
of limp sorries which still lie
in messy heaps filling rooms.

Throwing open the back door
she breathes air sown with frost
as upstairs the saxophone lets out
a series of discordant notes.

The few remaining cherries
and four get-well cards are in a bag
when Sue appears, face broken,
and flings her arms round Rebecca:

'Hospitals scare me to death
but I promise I'll drop in
and say hallo before the rehearsal.'

Rebecca hugs her. Both sob.
'We do communicate, don't we, Mum?'

Nine

Busy birdprints cover the snow
on the ice lidding the pond.
Stooping to feed bewildered ducks
and pick up broken glass, Steve remembers
he dreamt about Jade last night.

When he stands he's surprised to see her
braving the bitter park, wheeling
the Indian woman wrapped in a quilt.
For a moment he clutches at hope
but lets it go.

                    Face expressionless
as a drawn blind, she's heading
for the hothouse warmth, not him.
When he greets her she says fiercely:
'A treat for Surinder – flowers!'

He helps raise the heavy woman,
hovers while she defeats the step,
shuffles through the doors. He sees
the hollow brown face fill with joy.

Jade drops behind and he wishes
her pale hair was loose, not in a plait
beneath a scarf, wishes he could kiss
her lips roughened by the cold.

She whispers: 'Surinder came in today
with a bruise purple as a plum
on her palm and scratches on her neck.
She's in a terrible state but can't speak –
it's happened before. I know the signs:
her sister's family ill-treat her.'

The small space is tense with facts –
the distance between them, miles.
He longs to cross it, soothe, assist,
be admitted to her flat, her world again,
tries to follow

           the jumps from point
to point. Begins to get the gist:
Surinder had a tantrum, emptied
eight tins of paint, threw one
at a chair, tore drawings off a wall.

Trembling, Jade grasps his arm:
'The bloody director wouldn't recognize
she might be at risk, just bullshitted:
"She's become a danger at The Unit,
I'll write a report." Pig ignorant!'

Steve stares at the unsteady woman
oohing and aahing among the petunias,
laughing at banana leaves.
At sea he flounders for words,
mouths a useless sentence.
Jade thanks him for listening
as if neither link nor rift
had ever existed between them.

He gives Surinder a small pot
of primulas thick with buds.
Exuberant, she hugs it to her chest.
He watches as she's pushed past
trunks reddened by the dropping sun.

Back under glass he's angered
by a scattering of pulled petals
and two flowerheads on the floor –
but perhaps she was trying to gather
the bright colours. His feelings turn
to pity.

      As he moves the broken plants
he sees a moth on a slat, touches
its wings which are orange as pollen.

It crumbles and he remembers the end
of his dream: he'd stroked Jade's head
and her beautiful hair had fallen out.

Ten

She goes down corridors, steps,
through the maze of ill-assorted blocks
and huts that make up the hospital,
past heat steaming from vents,

out to the long street to suffer
sickly yellow lights, the bad breath
of trucks. But tonight none of this
overwhelms Rebecca.

      Tonight
she's holding tightly onto hope
bright and sharp as a new moon.

In the ward she'd found Thomas dressed
absorbed in reading the paper
and though he'd complained of a headache,
the food, lost his temper twice,

his delight as he tasted the cherries,
gingerly unwound crisp paper,
fingered the tip of a blue iris bud
sheathed like a baby in the womb,
had touched her to the quick.

And suddenly he'd remembered the hour
before the attack, six complex points
of an agenda. Almost his old self,
he'd instructed her to phone in.

Warmer than that self and close
to tears, he'd hugged her when she left,
mumbled: 'You're so patient, Rebecca.'
And she'd put his words away,
to treasure, to touch . . .

At the station criss-crossed bars
cage her in the ancient lift
with a skinny woman burdened by bags
who nods: 'Worser and worser!'
as they're plummeted through stale air

to the platform where Rebecca leans
against brown and dirty white tiles
until a poster across the rails
arrests her:

        'Constant criticism,
continual silent disapproval
are as cruel as beating a child.'

The words are written for her, spoken
to her. As if an arrow of light
had slanted through tall windows
her darkness is slit in two.

She sees her parents' stern shapes
magnified on the tunnel walls, hears
the whip in their voices, withholdings,
recognizes at last the wrongness
she's borne as long as she can remember.

Hundredweights shift, lift.
She feels again Sue's face wet
on hers and as the train rushes in
with silvers and ambers, distances open out.

Eleven

The room is full of silence.
Roses that were pink weeks ago
have dropped petals brown
as old menstrual blood on the piano.

Jade stares at a rusted self
hovering in the window, tugs curtains,
wishes the twins were at home.
Their phone calls, sweaty socks,
forgotten coffee mugs,
would paper over the hole made
by tearing Steve out.

                    She cuts bread,
shoves two slices under the grill.
It was unbearable bumping into him
in the park – feeling his longing,
wanting him, unhiving the angers
in her head to fend him off.

If only his sweet earnest face
didn't wear such vulnerability.
Like the glass house he's afraid
will be closed by council cuts
he reflects every glint, every cloud.
And he's exposed to June's weathers,
burning frosts –

          'Bugger!' She blows
on flames, butters blackened toast,
takes it to the studio, turns
the portrait of Surinder to the wall,

still seeing her swollen scratches
and eyes unfocussed by fear,
still hearing the director repeating
the letter of the law. Snorts to herself:
the brainless sod would tell Portia
the quality of mercy is unprofessional.

Pushing down an intractable fear,
she pours oil and turps
into metal cups, concentrates
on the dark limbs of a gymnast
she sketched in the heat of summer.

On the canvas the girl's legs
topped with golden shorts
bestride city streets, bridges,
a multi-storey park packed
with cars sleek as eggs.

Mixing river greens, violets
Jade is absolved of Surinder.
The ache for Steve, the hateful walls
of self, disappear.

                    Nothing exists
but five basic colours, the balancing
of shape and space, light with shade,
straight line with angle, curve.
Minutes slide into hours.

A persistent bee in her ear becomes
the phone. Steve? Why do without
because she can't have enough love.

Heart loud, she picks up the receiver.
A female voice: 'Would you believe –
I've sold it!' The disappointment
is so sharp she can hardly answer.

Twelve

'Red, red!' Surinder strokes
the crimson of Rebecca's shirt.
And Rebecca, wondering how someone
reduced to five words
and tiny patches of understanding,
can wear such joy,

                        sets out photos
of washing hands, ironing a shirt –
the small matter of everyday,
asks for *the woman waving*.

Surinder seizes the card, echoes it,
making farewell a fun ballet,
pounces on her other favourite,
a boy playing the flute, and hums.

Two years ago four actions flummoxed her.
Now she's quick to identify twenty-six.
While she fits pictures cut in two,

Rebecca imagines the scene she missed
this morning: Surinder emptying paints,
letting out sounds of rage,
thinks how mention of home
drives the light from her face. If only
she could speak her angers, fears.

A phonecall as the session ends:
Thomas, voice unsteady with excitement,
'They're letting me go tomorrow,'
then shouting: 'you're no use!'
when he can't decide which coat
he wants Rebecca to bring.

                              Wishing
she was alone in the iciness outside,
she calms him, cuts him off,
feels terrified she won't cope at home
with his demands, mood changes;

knows Sue will pout about the need
for quiet: 'I've got to practise –
go and buy Dad earplugs!'
Doors will bang, the house fill
with saxophone, explode
into words, jagged silences.

Weak-legged, Rebecca grasps a handrail
as beaks open to peck and peck her,
remembers the message on the poster,
forces the mouth points to shut,
hurries down a corridor.

She's signing thank you to a deaf man
who's given her a card he's made
when she sees Surinder.

                      Face frantic,
she is shoving boxes into her holdall
and hitting out at a new instructor
trying to retrieve them. Surprised,
he yells: 'Ouch, she's attacked me!' . . .

'People who are brain-damaged
do hoard possessions,' Rebecca
reminds the director in his office,
but he demolishes discussion:
'We can't cope with her here.'

Thirteen

Ice fissures, punched stars,
holes that will suck him in.
Appalled, Steve counts the panes
smashed in the night, bends
over poinsettias, fallen birds
lying among their crimson feathers.

A dream comes back from nights ago:
the hothouse shrunk to doll-size.
He'd hidden it beneath his bed
but June had nosed it out,
snubbed: 'Tacky white elephant,'
and kicked. His cries woke him.

Righting a plant, he imagines
the supervisor full-blown as a prophet
from the Old Testament, condemning
the hothouse to everlasting darkness.
Suppose he has the repairs done
in secret, pays from his own pocket?
The flimsy fantasy

               is blown away
by the supervisor rattling the door:
'Make sure our flower display
is absolutely tip-top next week –
a commercial's to be filmed in here.'
Puffed with his own importance
he hints at the high fee,
all the publicity.

            Glass grit
beneath his feet, mouth frozen,
Steve points at the broken panes.
'Get a glazier in at once –
I'll push the paperwork through.'

He should be relieved, elated
about the hothouse's new status,
but at the end of the morning
Steve walks the park feeling bleak
as the compacted mounds of grey snow
rising from flattened grass.

And he can't forget June's complaints:
her tea too weak, the marmalade
too coarse a cut, her crossness swallowed
by a torrent of words he had no idea
was roaring inside him, her face
as he left, a terrible white silence.

He's tending the plants flattened
in the night when he sees Jade
by the hothouse door. No wheelchair –
she's by herself.

         Not daring to think
she's come to find him, he asks:
'Where's your Indian lady?'

'Surinder? Caged in her sister's house.
Our fantastic director couldn't wait
to muster reasons for chucking her out.
In a few months she'll be ferried
once a week to an unsuitable centre.'

Steve's sense of oppression grows.
Unable to speak, he shakes his head.
'It's awful but I didn't come to moan.'
Jade's voice is suddenly soft as moth wings.
He could cry.

         'My self-portrait with the piano,
a small gallery's sold it – and I'm sorry,
will you forgive me for going berserk
that night?' Her mouth trembles.

'It's all right.' He touches her arm.
Tonight he'll let nothing stop him
from seeing her. June recedes.
Colour pours into the world again.

Fourteen

The morning is pale as if light
couldn't find the strength to rise,
and by three the afternoon's infected
with fast-spreading darkness.

When Rebecca leaves the Unit
day is lost and lamps are lumps
of harsh brightness that fail
to illuminate hollows in pavements,
darknesses between buildings
or the clot that lodged inside her
after the news that came by phone
of Surinder's fall in the night
down a flight of stairs,

                              her death
an hour after admission to hospital
from injury or another stroke,
her sister's snapped: 'She wanders,
I couldn't watch her all the time.'

Shut in her room with Jade, sandwiches
she couldn't eat, Rebecca had sobbed
into the *waving woman* card:
'There was something about her, a grace
that's so rare.'

                    And Jade had slammed:
'Four years ago she was a sister
on a psychiatric ward and called
The Angel – everybody's failed her.'

The wind is nagging shop signs
as Rebecca emerges from the Tube.
She keeps picturing Surinder's sister
whom she met once. No sign of love
in her shifting eyes, tinkling bangles.

But this is simplistic judgement.
She thinks of times she's felt afraid
Thomas would be dazed, frustrated,
demanding for the rest of his life,
and how a hatred of him welled up
then sank, leaving her ashamed.

Yet she can't rub out an image
of tentative feet at the crest of the stairs,
a silvered arm lifted, heavy tumbling,
blood dribbling from a soundless mouth.

Crying, she stumbles home,
struggles with her key and wet anorak.
Thomas sees she's upset, pours a brandy
and she can't help gabbling about Surinder –
her death, her life.

                    He doesn't glance
at the paper once, gives her all his attention
which she hugs like a comforting coat,
then grows expansive, instead of creeping
into herself, certain she's bored him.
He asks questions and warmth flows
through her: he seems to value her work.

Later, he talks of the blank place
where he was lost miles from memory,
his terror that his name was a label
wrongly attached and how stones
churning in his head ground the sense
out of words.

                    Holding him tightly
Rebecca knows he's himself again –
himself in a softer mould.

But in bed at the fuzzy edge
of sleep the day swims through her.
And she's holding a sack packed
with matter more destructive
than dynamite. How dispose of it safely?

Aching with the weight, she cranes
for the glittering shock of the sea
huge as childhood and very blue
against the horizon.

                Suddenly
she is in it and wading far out,
the restless animal surface
crinkling mother and father,
transfers peeled from her little book.

Letting go, she plunges into
clear green and mauve strata
where frilled streamers of seaweed

become people waving banners,
sea anemones are hearts swelling,
and the flower with spiky leaves
that laces her hands with blood,
is called Surinder. She hears Thomas
repeating her name, surfaces.

THE SOLITARY DOG

(after a painting by Paul Millichip)

for Shirley and Paul

I don't pick him out at first,
my eyes drawn to the hutch
of a house, its vanilla walls
peeling, ice-blue framing
the crude rectangular orifices
shut against light's shriek.

A line travelling the yard
is heaped with cloaks, covers,
dream materials tailing
the dust – as if the inhabitants
had emptied their small house,
hung out vulnerable selves.

Too voluminous for sheets
not dense enough for quilts,
these curtains wear blue-greens
culled from ocean dark
and purples lifted from Hades
to temper day's white heat.

'Fishing nets,' says Paul,
'dragged over the shore to dry'.
I enter the still layers
salt with centuries, am stripped
of pressures, wants, absences,
put on quiet's clothes.

Stooping, I pick brittle leaves,
flake them into dust, hear
a voice inside me insistent
as the sea's. Then I notice
that purposeful dog forever
trotting into indigo shade.

ABLUTIONS

(after 'Shower' by Les Murray)

Don't be fooled by the shower,
its snake head acting dead until a sizzling tongue delivers
a baptism of scald.
This is a religion of extremes.
You are pelted with cold scooped from Polar Caps,
your cage is drummed by a tribe of tropical beetles.
Stung into St Vitus's dance you soon slip on the molten soap
and with purple petalling your elbow
escape to the towel's dry safety.

Give me that quieter creed – the nightly bath:
an instant solution for icicle feet, absolution from stress,
half an hour slumped in Roman Empire indolence
dunking toes in foam and dreaming of palms on an island
hemmed with cinnamon sand and ocean lace,
an experienced lover who croons to buttoned shoulders,
a natural remedy for the back longing to be easy again.
No use in a room where bald walls exhale December.
At its best when heat gushes through silver arteries,
and leafy shadows shift pinkly on gleaming tiles.
In this pacific pool you lose sight of intractibles
as water covers your grassy patches, laps over dunes,
trickles into clefts, whispers to the inner rivers,
allows the timid self.
You lie watching anklets of liquid light, the far-reaching brush,
the slap-happy crab-coloured flannel, wrists and legs
co-operating without an agenda more amicably, more effectively
than any club committee, political party or group of nations.
And by this route you sail,
immaculate as Venus on her shell,
towards the coast which is tomorrow.

WOMAN IN THE BATH

(after a painting by Bonnard)

At first you're Ophelia –
belly, ribcage, whole being
sucked down. But your pale
lilac limbs, the autumn bush
of your head bloom in the water.

The fear hardening your flesh,
the fear chaining you to dim
stifling rooms, begins to liquify.
Terrifying compartments forget
partitions. The floor sprawls,
talks blue and mustard mosaics.
Tiles, let loose to the ceiling,
praise the garden: buddleia purple,
delphinium, chrysanthemum gold.

Beyond glass: those avenues
to emptiness, all their branches
that deny sky, pester wrists,
invade waist and thighs
are smoothed into silence.

Your small dependable dog
is a motif stamped on the mat.
The bath soft as kid, lip
folded back, will peel off
easily as an evening gown.
This dream of colourdots, daubs
is so persuasive it raises you
from the indelible sadnesses within
and you are scented with light.

FREEWHEELING

I press my bell, silver
the air, make cars
and battle-rattle lorries
melt into the river of tarmac.
Now my mood is flamingo-pink.

Darkness runs down the sky,
kisses the lamp post
into an ostrich. 'Bury your head,'
I sing. It winks and everywhere
is twinkle-twinkle-little-star.

Suddenly the seafront tugs
and I hurtle down stone flights.
At the bottom the Alsatian I love
is barking with joy, back
from a place I dared not imagine.

Once his owner whispered:
'Enemies put down poison –
he's been sent elsewhere,'
and I'd seen her flame curls
were unreal – a cheat, a wig;

knew she'd tucked out of sight
more than her hairlessness.
I croon to the dog who licks me,
twirls me by my gaberdine sleeve.
Buoyant I reach the esplanade,

find the pixie bonnet I threw
in the sea when I was five,
washed up on a rock shelf.
No life in the salt-dry
pink velour I hold to my face.

On the path of a strangely
risen sun I float out
beyond bucket and spade,
moorings undone. How my saddle
gleams with water jewels!

AN OLD STORY

First of all the unresisting infants
were laid out on a bed:
Claribel, her favourite, who won stars
for sums, a star of beauty herself
though her fawn snout and ears
were worn hairless from fondling,
and Patty Panda with human arms,
whom her small brother carried everywhere
in a basket that once held sweets.

Special too was the dainty lamb,
Nancy, whom someone rude had called
a ragged titch, Tony whose body
was bolster-shaped, and Meg Miller,
a pale flopper who had woollen pigtails
and was named after a friend
they had quarrelled with for ever.
Soon the Bad Ones set upon
the innocents, stripped them of clothes,

smacked their bottoms very hard,
dragged them crying from home,
dangled them over the terrible drop
from the banisters, let them fall
into the hall, kicked them into a gutter
where they lay wet and unwanted.
Secretly, the Bad Ones
fingered their nasty behaviour
and sniffed its deliciousness.

But the Angels, pink and smiling,
gathered up the little ones,
washed away their fear, dressed them
in knitted jumpers, warmed them
by a fire whose tongues licked gently,
lullabied them in the old dolls' pram.
The finale was always Christmas:
half a morning wrapping up
carefully chosen gifts in newspaper,

then the hot ribboning of excitement
as Claribel, Patty and the others
undid books, thimbles,
whispered words of gratitude.
The Angels drew out this ceremony
as long as they possibly could
as if they somehow knew
they would be trapped all too soon
in a world where they'd have no power
to create such satisfactions again.

UNDER

I wanted to funnel it
into one of those greywhite
cooling towers that stand
in wide blue sky
but I knew it wouldn't fit in.

I tried to lose it
in a forest's pathlessness,
to drown it in a swollen river
but I couldn't scrape it
from my skin, unscrew it
from my mind.

At home I worried it
into dry earth with a spade,
buried it beneath clods,
twigs, weeds, pieces
of willow-pattern plate.

But it remained inside me
and I was mouthless
as a rag doll,
its unending segments
dragging me down,

until I saw its bulk
seeping sawdust and slime
was my anger with you and you
who have closed your ears to me,
turned off your faces.

Then I picked up a stone
and stared at my feelings,
a redbacked army
seething seething
on its damp underside.

THE RED CUPBOARD*

is wide open. It is not rage
     that's ripening
in this recess. In the swell of heat
no bonfire flames are ripping
into wood. Linings and shelves
radiate cardinal, damson,
     coronation reds,
the utterness I long for daily.

The cool of vases, upturned glasses
     with quiet stems,
a plate propped on its rim affirm
the everyday. The small globes
could be transparent eggs,
egg-shaped apples. But the apples
     are weighty
as earthenware, shine like china.

Why am I feeding this passion
     for seeing
one thing as another: reflections
that throw light, intensify, extend
yet meddle with the original? I want
untouched, the apple-sweetness
     that sifts
through racks, lofts, hall passages.

---

* A painting by Bonnard

Impossible. Every apple
        I touch
is the alphabet's start, a wrinkled mouth,
the curve of a cheek that persists
from dream. And these on the shelf
are a tempting red, from the garden
        where Eve
picked, from all my gardens.

So where does it lead, this opening?
        To the night
under the stairs with cocoa, blankets,
no roughnesses to snag hands, nightie,
to an emptiness that will never
be filled, a cry that won't be answered.
        Yet inside
the red cupboard nothing is denied.

THE PANIC BIRD

That moment
when the mattress splits
and seeps its stuffing
when floors crack, roads
break up, ground gapes

that moment
when the breathstream
dries, the belly ceases
to exist and the self
can no longer hold on

that moment
when reason bolts
and six obsessive words
pound pound on the shell
of the emptied brain

is the moment
the wingspan spreads.
The predator descends,
traps hair, neck –
I am eclipsed.

I try to yell
for someone to put out
the rock-blue eyes,
smash the razor beak,
crush the claws,

Only a child
looms. Weightless as a leaf
she's crouched on a mountain ledge
whimpering: 'I can't bear
blood, illness, change.'

I want to
take her in my arms, struggle
to a safe place, outstare
the bird, seize it by the neck,
pull the gaudy feathers.

I want to
call out, voice belled
by fierce red joy, to alight,
toes touching waterbird
rings on lake calm.

THE PHOTOGRAPH

has fixed my mother and father in a garden
I know by heart though I've not entered it
for years. A sharper mirror than water, it insists
on their solidity, claims they will shine for ever.
As I look a longing I can't call love stops up
my throat and I'm shocked that each parent
is thinner than card, than one of the scrawled
white sheets lying on my desk – is nothing
I can touch in a rosebed labelled remembrance.
Yet here they sit on a gleaming bench, brighter
than life, presenting smiles to the world.
Her summer dress is dappled mauve and blue,
he's in his best suit, handkerchief peeping.
Behind them by the hedge with the iron-runged gate
I opened so often to dream among the raspberries
and broad beans, unrestrained phlox
offer exuberant heads . . .

'Don't be stupid!' My father's fist lands
on his spindly diagrams of electric circuits.
Spring is trying to climb in the window
and my sixteen-year-old self aches to jump
out to beech-leaf sunlight, out of disgrace
for not understanding, making undrinkable tea,
never sitting up straight at table. And now
my mother is slapping crockery into the sink
because he's too busy to go on a picnic.
Suddenly both are throwing bricks of rage
and that faint, wavering self pulls back
the screams threatening to leap from her head,
terrified she'll be struck into madness . . .

Banish these two, sink the garden?
I'd wipe out my path from then to now,
lose myself. I need to recover the time
when darkheart leaves, the wind running
through young wheatfields were too perfect
to bear, to recapture my mother playing the piano,
stooping to name a small flower on the Downs,
that walk from humming stubble heat into
the blur of evening when we were in tune
and she said: 'Your mind is beautiful'. I need to find
my father – the excitement we shared as he gave me
glimpses into the strange country of mathematics,
its patterns, laws, the invisible dimension occupied
by the square and potent root of minus one
which burgeoned wildly in my dreams at night. If I sit
with my parents on their bench will angers cease
and the soft salt waters of forgiveness rise?

RECUPERATION

Is it sanity dawning
after a long dishevelled night when you lay coughing,
hot and cold in a swaddle of blankets while each hour shoved
its ugly face into yours and owls ringed the dark? The slow
thinning of the greywhite fabric hung across the park
into a backdrop that's a luminous blue, the way
sipping tea loosens the pincer grip that's locked
your throat?

Is it Chopin swirling
from the transistor – that mazurka you practised all those years ago
when you retreated from rooms where voices scratched, clashed?
Remembering your velvet music teacher's words:
'Don't jump wrists: movement must always be curved'?
How the dead family house telescopes into your own home
as furniture, faces, defeat, dissolve in runs
and leaps of notes?

Tissues scrunched
and strewn over the bedroom floor, messy as emotion – is it that?
Removing the stale nightdress, the vest of sweat turning to shiver,
lowering the weak frame through steam that magically clears
nose, ears? Is it the kindness of water, a blessing
beyond everything but the moment of interleaving
body, mind with the one who knows
your terrible dimensions?

Simple as stopping, is it?
A sudden refusal to cram time like a shopping bag,
staying instead in the window bay to watch the noisy geese flap
in formation past the viaduct, past the crimson sun
hooked in a tree's claws? The way those three wrapped figures stride
over the stiff playing-field grass in the wake of a dog rushing
towards a speck in the squander of light –
the stillness after?

THE BLUE BALCONY

To open a door at the end of a journey,
be immersed in a dimness
that stills the pricking behind eyes,
unravels the tension in shoulders

to touch cotton covers on beds
indistinct as ebbing dreams,
be drawn to long gauze curtains
pale as flesh kept from sun,

part the easy wings, be cooled
by a faint scent of lavender,
before unpeeling the glass sheets
from slats needled with light;

to taste the promise of heat,
unfasten green shutters,
push them wide open onto
steep terraces of air –

is a yes to the leap in the belly
as possibility fans out
its fingers, and sky rushes in
with unstoppable blue.

     ★ ★ ★

South, this clarity –
intense as an insistent bell –
   must be South.
Have I emerged in a painting
or can I believe in this balcony,
   the shelving gardens
ending in a fierce drop to the sea,

the pink hats
on minute buildings along the bay?
I will go down, make sure
   the three palms,
one islanded in a blue pool,
the branches of hard green oranges,
   are not a mirage.

   To someone above
I shall only be a sunhatted blur
   as I take in
the immense violet calm
carrying small triangles of joy
   and funnels faint
as the stray beginnings of a thought.

★ ★ ★

Ice and lemon juice
in a glass on the white balcony table;
two chairs to arrange,
re-arrange, according to sun, shade.

Reclining on the striped canvas
I expect paradise as I taste the view,
its rise and dip of green and blue,
dramatic rocks. My book is open.

Beside me: sea thrift, succulents
straggling from a terracotta urn,
bougainvillaea clinging to a wall.
Parting the magenta clusters,

I uncover a thick dusk with petals
colourless as aged paper. In the shadow
the cool is suddenly a knife and I push
my chair into a pool of sun.

Heat bites into my neck. I shift
and shift until I find a balance,
know perfection will last
no more than moments but let go.

★ ★ ★

This gracious building, its carpets,
cooling passages, polished wood,
separate me from the mesh of everyday.
Through its windows I can make out
slopes, ridges, the mystery of cloud
forming, clearing, re-forming
over the mountain's jutting head.

Tomorrow I will set out
in sandals, brave the icy wind
bare-armed, grow breathless
in thin air, grasp rock knuckles
as I scramble upwards, press
my back against slate folds
in the fight to keep my balance.

This is the peak I have always
been aiming for. It doesn't matter
that the summit is unattainable.
I'll watch the thick steam gush,
gasp at the thought of the throat,
and the fire – oh the fire in the belly
will fill me with red ferment!

★ ★ ★

It lies below me,
blue unfolding on blue to
a white ever. Light hovers
on its surface; underneath
are calm islands of indigo.

It is gentle as fluent breath,
the breath I couldn't find
after the operation,
chest full of cough,
air scraping my throat,

the breath father fought
to keep in those four
final days of struggle.
I want this sea's quiet slide
from day to night to day,

wish it were possible
for me, for all of us
to leave as easily
as that small boat
passing far below.

Now it is a single leaf
in a watercolour,
a fly speck,
a full stop,
no more.

Reviewers on Myra Schneider's collection *Exits* (1994)

'Myra Schneider's poems are typically low key but rich with delays. And often these delays are really arrivals, intricately discovered, alight all over the room. She's not merely promising: she has herself arrived, and delivers.' – Les Murray

'*Exits* is Myra Schneider's fifth full collection and continues her characteristic perspective of setting in relief the significance of the everyday. Her work is sparked by observation, reflection and memory, rooted in the here and now. The openness of her subject matter is balanced by a restraint, a poise in the writing, which gives the particular a representative feel. Her vision is deeply humane, and accepting of vulnerability.' – Cynthia Fuller, *Writing Women*

'The paradox of belonging "with those who don't belong" reflects a theme – perhaps a key – that recurs throughout the ten years spanning her volumes. It has to do with a sense of being adrift and rootless in the world, yet at almost one and the same time being rooted and secure at home . . . One reviewer (Grevel Lindop) quotes Sydney Keyes in saying that her poems embody "some inkling of the continual fusion of the finite and infinite, spiritual and physical" and that surely is true.' – Keith Gilley, *The Inquirer*

'The title poem "Exits" is a profound poem written in an autobiographical style. There are many levels and meanings to the different sections: exits from "the Roundabout". . .' – Patrica Oxley, *Acumen*

'Myra Schneider's book *Exits* opens with a real cracker. "In The Beginning" is a funny, philosophical, and slightly off the wall account of breakfast over the morning papers . . . After that it's a surprise to come across the poems "Consider the Aubergine" and "Root Vegetable Stew". It's a confident poet who can shift between such diverse subjects as quantum physics and vegetables. Schneider does it with ease.' – Neil Rollinson, *The North*

Other books in the same series include

KEVIN CROSSLEY-HOLLAND *Poems from East Anglia*

MARTYN CRUCEFIX *A Madder Ghost*

HILARY DAVIES *In a Valley of This Restless Mind*

DAVID GASCOYNE *Encounter with Silence*

DAVID GASCOYNE *Selected Prose 1934-1996*

GARY GEDDES *Flying Blind*

PHOEBE HESKETH *A Box of Silver Birch*

JEREMY HOOKER *Our Lady of Europe*

NICKI JACKOWSKA *Lighting a Slow Fuse*

JUDITH KAZANTZIS *Swimming Through the Grand Hotel*

BLAKE MORRISON & PAULA REGO *Pendle Witches*

VICTOR PASMORE *The Man Within*

PASCALE PETIT *Heart of a Deer*

ANTHONY THWAITE *Selected Poems 1956-1996*

EDWARD UPWARD *Remembering the Earlier Auden*

EDWARD UPWARD *The Scenic Railway*

Please write to Enitharmon Press for a full catalogue